Original title:
Kisses at Sunset

Copyright © 2024 Creative Arts Management OÜ
All rights reserved.

Author: Holly Grant
ISBN HARDBACK: 978-9908-0-0516-4
ISBN PAPERBACK: 978-9908-0-0517-1

Romantic Echoes at Horizon's Edge

As the sun dips low, a slip of a grin,
We both chase shadows, what a silly spin!
Your laugh, a giggle, like bubbles of cheer,
I trip on my feet, oh dear, not again!

Evening's Embrace

The sky's a canvas, splashed with delight,
You pretzel my hair in the fading light.
We tango with seagulls, oh what a sight,
You'd think we were stars, in the soft twilight.

Moonlit Promises

Under the moon, my sandwich you stole,
You promise me laughter, not letting me roll.
With crumbs on your face, it's a comedy show,
My heart's in stitches, but I love you so!

The Last Ray of Warmth

As daylight wanes, my heart does a flip,
You splash in the puddles, oh take me on a trip.
With freckles on noses, and smiles that beam,
We wave to the stars, in a light-hearted dream!

Moments in the Dimming Light

As the sun dips low, we start to sway,
Mismatched socks, what a clumsy display.
You missed my lips and got my cheek,
Laughter erupts in the twilight peak.

The neighbors peep, oh what a sight,
Trying to catch a love made of light.
A dance with shadows, we twirl and trip,
A war of giggles with each little slip.

Embracing the Twilight Hour

In the twilight time, you pull me near,
But trip on your feet, oh dear, oh dear!
A playful dodge and a cheeky bite,
Who knew love was such a silly plight?

The broomsticks laugh at our crazy play,
As you whisk me around just a little too gay.
With a twirl so wild, you give a shout,
And land like a frog, we both break out!

Shades of Love Unfold

Under hues of orange and soft pink hues,
We laugh and tumble like we've had too much booze.
Your aim is off as you close your eyes,
A peck on the nose, what a big surprise!

The squirrels above are our only cheer,
As they nibble nuts while we giggle here.
A wink, a grin, oh watch out for bees,
Now dodging stingers, our hearts are at ease.

Golden Hour Whispers

As day turns to night, you steal a glance,
In moonlit mayhem, we join the dance.
A fumbled attempt to make sparks fly,
Accidental collision, oh my, oh my!

Your hair's in my mouth, what a sticky mess,
Laughing so hard, we forget the stress.
With arms akimbo, we hold onto fun,
In this goofy twilight, we've already won.

Starlit Promises

Under the sky, we giggle and sway,
With popcorn and dreams, we throw cares away.
You steal a bite, then pretend it's all mine,
As we glow like the moon, oh, aren't we divine?

The stars begin winking, quite cheekily so,
Your hair's in my drink—oh no, such a show!
We laugh as we spill more than just our delight,
Two clowns at the dusk, dancing on through the night.

Gentle Touches at Day's End

The sun dips low, with a cheeky grin,
I nudge you gently, watch the fun begin.
You swipe at my ice cream, I swipe back the fries,
We giggle like kids, beneath the bright skies.

We talk about unicorns, if they were real,
What a sight they'd be, oh, what a great deal!
But then your shoe's squeaking, just like a cat,
And laughter erupts, it seems, just like that.

Velvet Horizons

The twilight wraps us in a cuddly hug,
With soda and snacks, we give each a shrug.
Your hand slips right into the buttery bowl,
Oh, the drama unfolds, we've lost all control!

We whisper our secrets as the sky turns gold,
You swear that your socks have a story untold.
But what's more important? Our laughter or light?
As dusk turns to mystery, we giggle with glee, all bright!

Secrets Shared at Sundown

Behind closed lids, the sunset starts fading,
With your crazy dance moves, my patience is fading.
You trip on a shoelace, fall right on your rear,
But instead of a frown, there's only good cheer.

With drinks in our hands and crumbs on our face,
We declare ourselves champions of silliness race.
As stars twinkle in, we make silly bets,
On who'll fall asleep first, oh, no regrets!

Celestial Unions

Two ducks in a row, they quack away,
Chasing the twilight as night starts to play.
One slips on a cloud, oh what a mess!
They laugh at the stars, all dressed up to impress.

A comet zooms past with a wink and a grin,
"You can catch me, dear friend, but only with spin!"
The moonlight giggles, as shadows collide,
While fireflies dance, in the warm evening tide.

Lullabies of a Dimming Day

A squirrel on a branch starts to whittle a tune,
Eyes on the horizon, he hums to the moon.
His buddy the owl falls asleep on a log,
"Wake up, my fine feathery fog!"

The stars yawn wide, but can't fall asleep,
Whispering secrets while the crickets leap.
A hedgehog nearby tries to snooze with flair,
But giggles erupt, floating into the air.

Radiance in the Reverie

A penguin in shades, sipping soda on high,
Raises a toast to the colors that fly.
His pals, in a huddle, all wink and they say,
"Let's paint the world blue before it turns gray!"

With splashes of laughter and sprinkles of light,
Their party erupts as day blinks goodbye.
Ice cream cones melt, but they don't seem to care,
As bubbles go popping, they dance in the air.

The Quiet Conclusion

As the day breathes out, a breeze starts to teasingly sway,
A cat in a hat spins tales of the fray.
Whiskers and giggles collide on the ground,
With each silly story, more laughter is found.

The world starts to dim, yet spirits stay bright,
A parade of the odd, all basking in light.
With one final snigger, the curtain comes down,
And the sun calls it quits, offering a frown.

Whispers of Twilight

In the waning light they prance,
A clumsy two-step, what a chance!
With giggles floating in the breeze,
They stumble, giggle, hearts at ease.

A poke, a nudge, a playful spin,
They chase the shadows, grinning wide.
With painted skies, their laughter rings,
Under the glow, joyfully they glide.

Each glance a joke, each smile a tease,
The world slows down, just like the seas.
In that moment, the day is done,
Two silly hearts, perfect for fun.

As twilight wraps them, colors blend,
Mischief dances, never to end.
With every hug and every cheer,
They twirl together, year after year.

Embrace Beneath the Dusk

Amidst the shadows, they start to twirl,
Laughing loudly, what a whirl!
Their hats askew, a shoe misplaced,
In sweet chaos, love is laced.

A flick of the hair, a playful poke,
The air is filled with playful smoke.
They keep it light, no burdens here,
Just goofy grins and silly cheer.

With every hug, a pratfall near,
Their giggles echo, loud and clear.
The sky blushes as night draws near,
With whispers soft, drawing them near.

Together they leap with joyful grace,
Creating memories in this space.
As twilight dances with their joy,
In this embrace, hearts won't annoy.

The Last Light's Caress

Beneath the clouds, they take their stand,
With sandwiches and drinks in hand.
A crust of bread, a ruckus made,
Their humor bright with sunset's shade.

A playful wink, a stretched-out arm,
Tickles and laughs, their silly charm.
With eyes that twinkle, cheeks aglow,
They pace the shore with a silly show.

As the sun dips low, they share a snack,
With crumbs on noses, there's no lack.
A sudden breeze, a gust of fun,
Their laughter echoes, two become one.

The final rays like whispers dance,
In this vibrant, clumsy romance.
With a final scoop of ice cream pink,
They steal a moment, and then they wink.

Lovers in the Fading Glow

Amidst the hues of orange and red,
Two lovers laugh, no words unsaid.
With silly faces, they take the plunge,
In a sunset race, both hearts will lunge.

A tumble here, a stumble there,
With sticky hands, they do not care.
Their giggles spread like butterflies,
Painting laughter across the skies.

In every hug, a playful tease,
Waltzing freely with youthful ease.
The fading glow, a warm embrace,
In this twilight, they find their place.

As shadows merge and twilight sings,
They dance like wind, on feathery wings.
Two goofy hearts, under the show,
In love's own humor, forever they grow.

Where Day Meets Night

As day drifts down, a silly plight,
Two squirrels chase, like lovers in flight.
They stumble and fall, make quite a mess,
Under the sun's warm, playful caress.

A shadow looms, a playful cat leaps,
Mocking the dance, as the twilight creeps.
Chasing their tails, laughter fills the air,
Nature's own show, with antics to share.

The sky ablaze with blush and cheer,
A twilight giggle, the end draws near.
A wink from the stars as laughter swells,
Where day meets night, all's well that dwells.

Themes of Heartfelt Farewells

A rubber duck floats, lost in the tide,
As friendships part, with quirks they bide.
Hats fly off, as breezes roam,
In this goodbye, they'll make it home.

With pinky swears and laughter's whim,
As time slips past, the light grows dim.
They juggle goodbyes, like clumsy clowns,
In heartfelt farewells, they wear their crowns.

The sun gives a grin, it's bound to rise,
But first, a chuckle, a few surprise cries.
For every sweet exit, there's joy in glee,
In parting, they find their next jubilee.

Allure of the Dusk's Palette

Orange and purple paint the sky,
With crayons misplaced, oh me, oh my!
Dips in laughter as day shakes hands,
The palette spills, like glittering bands.

A penguin strolls, with grace so meek,
Waddling proud, it gives a cheeky peek.
The allure of dusk brings forth its charms,
In this funny dance, it's safe from harms.

Fireflies flash like tiny bees,
Chasing the dusk with a buzzing tease.
As colors blend in the playful ride,
Night struts in, with a giggle of pride.

Threads of Night's Embrace

Stitches of stars twinkle and weave,
As the moon grins wide, it won't leave.
A blanket spun from laughter and dreams,
In night's embrace, it delights and beams.

The crickets croon a silly tune,
Beneath a sky, where wishes swoon.
These threads of night, a fabric bright,
With laughter stitched, they glimmer light.

A dance of shadows, pirouettes galore,
As the night whispers secrets and more.
In this silly twirl, they find their grace,
Through the playful threads of night's embrace.

Passion Beneath the Evening Sky

As the sun dips low, the squirrels do play,
They chase their tails, in a funny ballet.
Two lovers giggle, the moment's just right,
One trips on a shoe, what a silly sight.

With a wink and a grin, they share a sweet jest,
He whispers a line that he thinks is the best.
She rolls her eyes, yet she can't help but laugh,
As the fireflies join in, a quirky giraffe.

Their snacks get mixed up, popcorn flies in the air,
A butterfly lands on her unruly hair.
They muster a toast with cups full of cheer,
But the lemonade spills, oh dear, oh dear!

As they wipe the mess with a giggly flair,
Night wraps around, and they breathe in the air.
In the silliness, love blooms like a flower,
With each laugh shared, they savor the hour.

Hues of Love's Embrace

Underneath the pink, the clouds start to dance,
Two friends decide it's the time for romance.
He pulls out a blanket; it's frayed at the seam,
"We'll sit here and watch!" was his brilliant dream.

But ants have a plan and swarm for a feast,
Nearby they find crumbs from the last picnic beast.
Both jump with a squeal, a hilarious sight,
As they wave arms wildly, what a crazy flight!

With fruit and some cheese, all awkwardly placed,
She chuckles with glee, at the mess they embraced.
He tries for a bite but falls into goo,
Now sticky and sweet, they laugh till they spew.

As the sun bows down, they can't catch a breath,
Love wrapped in laughter feels alive, not a death.
They mark this wild evening with fun and some glitz,
In shadows of twilight, it's real, it's pure bliss.

Warmth of the Setting Sun

On the shore where the waves tease the sand,
A pair start to fumble as they both take a stand.
He spills his drink, causing quite the ruckus,
She bursts into laughter, says, "You're such a fuss!"

A seagull swoops down with a watchful eye,
Imitating romance, it steals fries from the sky.
With an exaggerated gasp, she says, "Oh no!"
But is met with a giggle, the playful show.

The horizon ignites in a fiery glow,
She leans in for a photo, but wait—oh no!
A wave crashes hard, and the camera goes sploosh,
Now memories are soggy—what a goofy truth!

In the midst of mishaps, they find their delight,
Wrapped up in laughter that lasts through the night.
As the stars twinkle on their too-salted chips,
Their humor, their warmth—akin to sweet sips.

Glimmers of Heartfelt Moments

As evening falls softly, the crickets all cheer,
A picnic of laughter while the skies start to clear.
With sandwiches flying and drinks gone astray,
They laugh till their bellies just ache from the play.

He tries to impress her with tales that are tall,
But sneezes through laughter—what a vibrant call!
She points at a bird, a clown in the air,
As it swoops down low, they attempt not to stare.

Their toes in the sand find the warmth of sweet sun,
But a tickling crab gives them both quite the run.
They tumble with giggles and shrieks fill the night,
The glimmers of joy make the sunset feel bright.

With blush on their cheeks and splashes of fun,
In the moment, they feel like the only two one.
In laughter, they swim through this magical blend,
As hearts in their laughter break every trend.

Evening's Caressing Touch

When the sun starts to yawn,
And the shadows begin to play,
We giggle like kids at the park,
Under skies that are turning gray.

The ice cream drips on my shirt,
As you steal a bite from my cone,
Your laughter dances in the breeze,
In this world, we feel right at home.

The clouds wear a gold crown,
While our jokes float around in the air,
Every chuckle a soft embrace,
As day whispers, 'Please, let's not care.'

With each wave crashing ashore,
We trip over shoes in the sand,
Your silly face makes me burst,
In this glow, oh so unplanned.

Laughter in the Golden Hour

In the warmth of the fading glow,
We dance like no one is near,
You twirl like a dizzy little bee,
While I'm laughing, holding my beer.

The cats gather to watch our show,
With eyes that are wide with surprise,
As we sketch silly shapes in the air,
Under peach skies, our fun never dies.

Your hair sticks up like a crown,
As I try to avoid a stray flip,
But laughter echoes through the dusk,
Not a single line can we skip.

As the last sliver slowly dips,
Our shenanigans echo like glee,
Just two goofballs in a sunset,
Together, forever carefree.

Bonding Under Fading Light

Under the sky draped in blush,
We play tag with the last of the sun,
Your silly dance makes me chuckle,
As we race, oh what a fun run!

The warm breeze carries our giggles,
As we sneak a peek at the moon,
You trip, and we burst into laughter,
Dawn will come far too soon.

With the fireflies doing their dance,
We compete to catch one on the fly,
Though our nets are made from our hands,
In this game, oh how we comply.

As the world wraps in shadows deep,
I whisper secrets you'll never tell,
In this fading light of the evening,
We find our joy, everything is swell.

The Last Light's Caress

The final rays tease the horizon,
As we strut like peacocks around,
You crack jokes about silly things,
And your laughter is my favorite sound.

With our ice tea glasses clinking,
We toast to the moments we own,
The fireflies playing hide and seek,
While we squint at the twinkling throne.

As the sky turns a mischievous pink,
Your hat flies off, oh what a sight!
We chase it down, just like kids,
In this playful plot of the night.

With hearts as light as the night air,
We whisper dreams of tomorrows bright,
In this glow, no worries at all,
Just laughter and love, pure delight.

Affection in the Fading Light

In the glow of evening's tease,
We lean in like we're trying to sneeze.
Lips misfire, a comical clash,
A peck on the cheek, oh what a splash!

Laughter echoes, the night takes flight,
Your nose bumping mine, what a sight!
With every giggle, the stars align,
Tonight, my friend, you are divine!

Twilight's Tender Embrace

As the sky blushes pink, we stand,
Counting the awkwardness, hand in hand.
Your hair gets tangled, my glasses mist,
In the haze, oh, how we've missed!

The sun dips down, a cheeky pang,
You whispered sweetly, then accidentally sang.
With a twist of fate and a wink from fate,
We staggered in love, it's never too late!

Love's Glow at Eventide

With the day's end, the antics begin,
You aim for my lips, but hit my chin!
Winks exchanged, like fish out of water,
Your "oops" makes my heart feel hotter!

As shadows dance and laughter spills,
Your feigned charm gives me the chills.
In twilight's grasp, we struggle and sway,
Two clowns, we laugh, as night steals the day!

Starlit Promises

Under starlight, a whispered joke,
We quiz the universe, "Is this love or smoke?"
My funny face makes you burst out loud,
While the stars above seem rather proud!

As the light dims, our hearts collide,
We fumble about, but take it in stride.
With a nudge and a laugh, I misstep to you,
Together we shine in this eccentric view!

A Dance of Shadows

Two shadows tango in the glow,
Tripping over toes with a show.
Laughter spills on the soft, warm air,
As they bump, giggle, and spin without care.

The sun dips low, a golden ball,
They misstep, but they're having a ball.
Caught in the thrill of twilight's cheer,
With each silly spin, the end draws near.

Lips zapped with whispers of grape-flavored fun,
Making funny faces as they run.
Their dance turns wild, a chaotic ballet,
While the sun sets down, bidding the day.

As night wraps up the dance they portray,
They bow and trip, in a comical way.
Upside down, with goofy grins, they run,
The curtain falls on their sunset fun.

The Evening's Tender Embrace

In the arms of evening, antics start,
With pizza crumbs and a cheesy heart.
Mouths adorned with sauce and zest,
They share a laugh, feeling quite blessed.

As the light fades, they pull off a trick,
A hotdog dance that's funny and slick.
With mustard mustaches and ketchup flair,
They twirl like clowns without a care.

The breeze, a giggle in their ear,
As they boast of victories, bold and sheer.
Witty quips harmlessly pursued,
In this glowing hour, life feels renewed.

With their soft murmurs and playful tease,
They find affection in moments like these.
Beneath a sky tinted pink to the core,
They laugh together, then laugh some more.

Silhouettes Against the Dimming Sky

Two dark shapes stretch in evening light,
Arms flailing madly in delight.
Cackling faintly, the shadows play,
As watchers giggle at their ballet.

One pretends to fly, quite absurdly bold,
While the other mimics a lion, uncontrolled.
They leap and tumble, a comical sight,
Under the canvas of fading light.

With each hop, a tiny yelp,
Twisting and turning, they can't help.
Against the dusk, their antics roam,
Creating chaos far from home.

As stars peek out, feeling quite shy,
They share their triumph with a sigh.
In the art of laughter, they're both winners,
Creating memories, like the best of dinners.

Soft Murmurs in Golden Hues

In a whirl of giggles on this rosy Eve,
Chewy candies make them weave.
With silly voices and playful chime,
They serenade the setting time.

A slip on a rock, oops, down they go,
Arms flail like windmills, oh what a show!
Squeals of laughter erupt from their hearts,
As their antics turn into funny parts.

The sun melts gently, sweet caramel glow,
As they bet on who can do the bottle flip show.
With candy-sticky fingers, they cheer and they tease,
As they sneak a bite of forbidden cheese.

The laughter lingers, a joyful spark,
In the twilight hush, their jokes leave a mark.
With every silly tale, as darkness looms,
They wrap up the day in whimsical blooms.

Night's Enchanted Whispers

The moon's a shy thief, with a grin so wide,
Stealing soft giggles where secrets hide.
Stars wink like mischief, wrapping us tight,
In the glow of the dusk, our laughter takes flight.

With firefly dances, we twirl like fools,
Chasing silly shadows and breaking old rules.
The night plays a tune, a silly little rhyme,
As we trip on our toes, making clumsy time.

In the midst of the giggles, a breeze sweeps near,
Tickling our noses, igniting a cheer.
Oh, how the twilight tickles the soul,
With whimsical wonders that make us feel whole.

So here's to the mess, the laughter, the fun,
In this silly ballet where hearts come undone.
In nights filled with whispers, we'll harmonize fate,
With snorts and with smiles, oh, isn't it great?

The Warmth of Our Shadows

Two shadows are dancing beneath the bright sun,
Their rhythm is clumsy, but oh, such fun!
We trip on our laughter, we roll on the ground,
With silly confessions that echo around.

A breeze carries whispers, we chase them with glee,
Like butterflies flapping, oh, wild and free!
In this awkward embrace, we slip and we sway,
With the light-hearted fire that brightens the gray.

Oh, how we misstep with our clumsy parade,
Spinning in circles, the world feels so played!
As the shadows grow long, and the sun starts to fade,
We giggle together, the fun never strayed.

So let's keep on dancing till stars dot the skies,
With mischievous grins and joyful surprise!
Each twirl and each whirl, a dance that we'll share,
In this goofy ballet, unaware or a care.

Owls and Starlight Whispers

Two owls conspire in the trees up high,
With beady-eyed wisdom, they watch us fly.
Under a blanket of twinkling delight,
We stumble on dreams in the hush of the night.

In a world full of giggles and silly old tales,
Our hearts fill with laughter like runaway sails.
The stars throw a party, we're the silly guests,
With jokes that ignite and put smiles to the test.

The moon asks for stories, we spin them with flair,
With every punchline we tumble through air.
And while owls roll their eyes in the moon's quiet glow,
We laugh like the mad ones, just go with the flow.

Each whisper of starlight wraps us in fun,
As we're caught in this magic till the night has undone.
In the chorus of owls, we find our sweet tune,
With laughter that echoes beneath the bright moon.

Harmonies of Heartbeats

In the twilight's embrace, our hopes start to sing,
As if captured by melodies that laughter can bring.
With quirky chimes echoing off trees so stout,
Our harmonies whisper, there's never a doubt.

With cheeks all a-flush, and giggles in flight,
We weave through the twilight, hearts dancing in light.
Every beat is a jest, every sigh is a cheer,
As fireflies join in, spreading joy and good cheer.

A sprinkle of chaos when we forget the steps,
We crash into dreams, it's the best of concepts!
With stars as our audience, we'll laugh and collide,
Creating our melody, a whimsical ride.

So let's serenade twilight with verses of bliss,
In a dance that's our own—it's a riot, not miss!
With heartbeats in harmony, we're silly and free,
Lost in the laughter—oh, what joy it can be!

Serenade of Shadows

In the fading light, we dance with glee,
Tripping over shadows and a bumblebee.
You tried to steal a sip of my drink,
But ended up with a splatter, don't you think?

We laughed as the colors swirled in the sky,
You made a funny face, oh me, oh my!
Your hair was a mess, like a bird in flight,
Yet your smile shone louder than the fading light.

The sun dropped low, and I grabbed a snack,
You thought it was a blanket—oh what a knack!
We tumbled in laughter, rolling on grass,
Daring each other to let the moment pass.

With the final glow, and the stars peeped in,
You said, 'Next time, I'll bring my violin!'
I snorted in laughter, what a laughable tune,
As we chased the fireflies beneath the moon.

Caress Beneath the Horizon

With our goofy grins painted in sunset hues,
You took my hand, said, 'Let's avoid the snooze!'
We leaped over puddles, slipped on our feet,
The horizon chuckled, our little duet sweet.

As the sky glowed orange, like a giant peach,
You tried to catch butterflies, or so you would teach.
But ended up chasing a squirrel or two,
Squirrels giggled back; who knew they could boo?

The breeze played gently, ruffling your hair,
I offered a snack, you just gave me a stare.
With crumbs on your nose, looking quite the sight,
We twirled in the twilight; oh what pure delight!

With one silver laugh, and an attempt to wink,
You knocked over my drink—and what did you think?
We both erupted in fits of delight,
This silly serenade, oh what a night!

Crimson Sky Affection

As the crimson hues splashed, we both stood still,
You looked like a painting, a bit of a thrill.
But then you tripped on a root, oh dear me,
Fallen like autumn leaves, under our tree.

We watched as the sun sank, oh what a sight,
You yelled at a bird that stole your last bite.
With each silly quarrel and playful shout,
We made memories worth more than gold, no doubt.

With a flicker of stars, we tossed silly dreams,
You claimed you could fly, or so it seems.
I said, 'You can't soar, you just ate too much!'
And we both burst out laughing; oh what a touch!

As night rolled in with its twinkling flair,
You promised me secrets with your wild hair.
But only a snort escaped from your lips,
Forgotten were tickets to our moonlit trips.

Soft Murmurs at Dusk

The twilight drew near with a mischievous grin,
You whispered your secrets, I just couldn't win.
We tripped on our tales, sharing giggles and sighs,
In a world where we thought we could touch the skies.

The evening descended like a sleepy cat,
I offered you snacks, as you danced in a hat.
You looked rather silly, but I must confess,
In a sunset glow, you wore it with zest.

With shadows as friends, we plotted a scheme,
To catch the last rays, like a playful dream.
You pretended to swim in an invisible sea,
And I couldn't contain my laughter, oh me!

As the stars sparkled, we shared silly tales,
Of pirates and monkeys and wind in our sails.
With the world around fading, as laughter arose,
We found joy in the dusk, as the cool evening froze.

Heartbeats in the Twilight

The sun dips low, a golden fry,
We giggle as fireflies wave goodbye.
With stolen looks and cheeky grins,
We dance like fools, where laughter begins.

Your hair's a mess, my shirt's a stain,
We blame the sunset, not the champagne.
With every laugh, a heart does race,
A silly spin in this wild chase.

So here we are, the sky awash,
Trying not to fall while we nosh.
A clumsy twirl, a playful trip,
Laughter spills like a sweet, fizzy sip.

Underneath the blush of sky,
We share our secrets, you and I.
A wink, a nudge, the night takes hold,
Let's be the legends in tales bold.

Solstice of Souls

The day is done, let's misbehave,
Running wild like kids, oh, we crave!
With lemonade smiles and spritzed-up tunes,
We moonwalk across the drift of dunes.

You steal a sip while I roll my eyes,
The sunset echoes with our soft sighs.
A starlit mess where wishes collide,
We're the jokes on the moon, what a ride!

So hand me your hat, I'll wear it tall,
A sunflower crown, like that's not a fall!
We face the tide, chasing swirling foam,
Who knew twilight was our love's home?

With tousled hair and pockets of dreams,
We blend in colors, or so it seems.
As darkness wraps us in its warm cloak,
We giggle lightly, sharing a joke.

Passionate Glances at Dusk

As the sky blushes, we take our stand,
With soda pop sounds and ice cream in hand.
You throw a wink, I return the tease,
This game of love brings sweet, breezy ease.

Under the clouds that purr and sigh,
We share our stories, let the time fly.
A laugh escapes, oh, what a scene,
Finding joy in silly routines.

So let's spin 'round till our heads are dizzy,
With sugary snacks that feel quite frizzy.
Two shadows dance on this path of gold,
In the twilight, our secrets unfold.

Your smile's a riddle, a raucous charm,
In this twilight grip, we feel so warm.
As the day softly waves, we make a pact,
In this merry moment, we won't look back.

The Palette of Our Affection

Splashes of orange, strokes of pink,
We paint the sky as we laugh and wink.
With each spilled color, a giggle erupts,
Like painters lost in our crafty hiccups.

A dab of chaos, a touch of grace,
There's joy in every brush of our face.
Mixing our thoughts with each crazy twist,
In these silly moments, we can't resist.

You chase the hues, I follow the light,
With polka-dot dreams all through the night.
We mix our laughter with shades so bright,
Creating a canvas of pure delight.

As the stars paint the night, we hold on tight,
In the art of love, we're the perfect sight.
With each stroke shared, a masterpiece made,
In this sunset world, where moments don't fade.

Sunlit Promises

In the park where laughter blooms,
We traded snacks and silly tunes.
Your chipmunk cheeks, a sight to see,
I laughed so hard, you spilled your tea.

Sunshine danced upon your face,
We made our plans, a wild chase.
You swore you'd fly, a paper kite,
But tangled up, you lost the fight.

Ice cream dripped, our shoes were sticky,
We chased a bug; it felt so tricky.
With each silly, awkward dance,
We sealed our fate, not left to chance.

So here's to hope, and dreams so bright,
In every laugh, we'll find our light.
Sunlit promises, hand in hand,
A goofy love, so unplanned.

Moonlit Wishes

Under the stars, we made a pact,
You wished for chips, I wanted snacks.
Your wobbly dreams, oh what a sight,
A lizard dressed in silver light.

We threw our hopes at the glowing moon,
You strummed your tune on a rusty spoon.
The neighbors peeked, with curious eyes,
As we launched jellybeans to the skies.

One slippery step and down you went,
But laughter echoed; joy was sent.
With gummy bears collecting dust,
In moonlit wishes, we both trust.

The night held secrets, dreams so wild,
You laughed and danced, a giddy child.
With every giggle, we danced 'til dawn,
In our silly world, we both belong.

Under the Veil of Dusk

As the sky turned a soft blush hue,
We played hide-and-seek, just me and you.
The whispers of dusk, they played our song,
But you tripped on shadows, oh so wrong!

Under the veil of fading light,
Your goofy grin was quite the sight.
You tried to run, oh what a feat,
But the pavement met your dancing feet.

We spun 'round like dizzy toys,
In laughter shared, we found such joys.
The trees applauded as you swayed,
With every misstep, our fears delayed.

So here's to clumsiness in the night,
Each stumble, a spark in fading light.
Under the veil, our silly sprites,
Together we danced, our hearts took flight.

Colors of a Shared Heartbeat

On a canvas painted with wild zest,
We mixed our dreams, a vibrant quest.
You splattered blue with a cheeky grin,
And yelped aloud, "Where do I begin?"

Colors swirled with a big surprise,
As we crafted giggles, beneath bright skies.
Your brush escaped with every splash,
Creating giggles in a playful crash.

Purple splatters, oh what a mess!
We painted love, I must confess.
Each hue reflected our goofy start,
Woven together, a shared heartbeat art.

In shades of joy, we found our fun,
With every stroke, two hearts as one.
Colors of laughter, bright and free,
In our silly world, just you and me.

A Canvas of Affection

The sky turns red like a ripe tomato,
We giggle, pretending to hold a ratio.
Painted clouds with splashes of glee,
Our smiles are the brush, wild and free.

A squirrel zooms, what a comical sight,
As we plot our escape, giggling in flight.
With each tiny breeze, a tickle we find,
Our laughter echoes, as we unwind.

The sun dips low, it's a goofy show,
We chase shadows, and dodge to and fro.
With ice cream cones, and sticky little hands,
We map out adventures, making grand plans.

In the fading light, we dance with the flies,
As twilight wraps us under its ties.
The world turns wacky, but we don't mind,
In this silly moment, true joy we find.

Vows in Twilight's Glow

In the glow of dusk, with twinkling eyes,
We vow to grab snacks and dodge the spies.
With chips and dip, our fortune revealed,
Adventures await, and laughter is healed.

Silly promises of pizza on toast,
We declare to the stars, with a giggling boast.
The night's soft blanket, in colors of cream,
Fills our hearts with the silliest dream.

Fireflies pop like balloons in delight,
As we twist and twirl into the night.
We joke about owls and their hooty debates,
While making our way past some prickly crates.

Underneath stars, we share a great laugh,
Winging it wildly, just like a giraffe.
Promises whispered, in a soft playful tone,
In this quirky dance, we feel right at home.

Evening's Covering Caress

The evening wraps us in a quirky embrace,
With wings of color, we start our race.
Against the backdrop of a blueberry hue,
We mime silly stories, just me and you.

A turtle strolls by, on his way home,
We cheer him on as he takes to the foam.
With chuckles and shrieks, our joy overflows,
As evening's caress tickles our toes.

The moon is a cheese ball, big and round,
We crack up at jokes, the silliest found.
As shadows dance, we write our own play,
With laughter and love lighting the way.

A breeze comes by, it's a ticklish tease,
We shuffle and laugh, as we float with ease.
In this whimsical world, an odd happily-ever,
We find joy in sunsets, light as a feather.

Flickers of Firefly Dreams

In the dusky glow, our dreams take flight,
With fireflies circling, what a funky sight!
We chase them around like kids on a spree,
Turning the night into a sparkling sea.

The glow of the stars, we pretend they chat,
As we jest and prance, and play with the cat.
A blanket of giggles covers us warm,
While embracing the chaos, it seems like a charm.

We sketch funny faces, with shadows so bold,
Each silhouette tells a story untold.
Our laughter erupts like a bottle of fizz,
Creating a world of humorous bliss.

In the twilight's arms, we waltz with our dreams,
With twinkling eyes and playful themes.
The night whispers secrets, of giggles and beams,
In our flickering hearts, we plot silly schemes.

Gentle Tides of Evening

As the sun dips down low, we should pay,
My hair's a wild mess, what do you say?
You call it romance, I just call it luck,
Your lips hit my cheek—hey, watch out for the duck!

The sand is warm, the sea gently sighs,
With sticky ice cream dripping, I cannot lie.
You try to look suave, but you trip on your feet,
And we both burst out laughing—oh, what a treat!

Seagulls circle above, making quite the scene,
While you declare your love with an ice cream cone sheen.
I can't help but smile, as you offer a bite,
But just then, I slip—oh, what a delight!

So here's to our evening, full of giggle and roar,
With waves as our witness, and sand on the floor.
You take my hand, and with a silly grin,
We make all the memories; this is how we win!

Love Letters in the Twilight

Beneath the glow of fading light, oh dear,
You've written me poetry, but I can't quite hear.
You sigh and you scribble with wild, crazy flair;
One word is 'giraffe'—did you pull it from air?

We giggle at shadows that dance on the sand,
You try to be suave, but you drop your handstand.
With half-formed love letters laced with some cheese,
This night is ridiculous, oh, how we tease!

The stars start to twinkle, as we make a pact,
To treasure each moment, just like a fun act.
You promise me chocolate, or maybe a dance,
But first, let's avoid that crab with a glance.

So here in twilight, we celebrate us,
With laughter and dreams—oh, it's a must.
You lean in for more, but seriously, wait!
You've got whipped cream on your face—such a fate!

Reflections of Shared Moments

As the horizon blazes, we share silly grins,
Your hat flies away—oh, where do I begin?
Chasing after it, you trip on the beach,
Rolling in laughter, just out of reach.

The mirrors of water, they show us so bold,
With our ice cream mustaches, and jokes that are old.
You narrate a story, it's wild and absurd,
With plot twists of fish—hold on, we heard?

The sun winks at us, as we hold our sides,
With echoes of laughter that never subsides.
We dance like the crabs, with moves quite uncanny,
And when I call you 'fisherman,' you say, 'Just a granny!'

So let's capture this moment, forever it stays,
In the book of our lives, filled with humorous plays.
With every shared glance, it's clear why it's fun:
You're the best date ever, and our laughter's my sun!

The Palette of Our Embrace

In this canvas of twilight, we mix up our hues,
You pull out the paint, but it's in such a ruse.
Pinks, yellows, and blues, what a sight to behold,
But wait, did you just mix a blob of mold?

We smear and we splatter, it's chaos with flair,
Your brush hits my nose; oh, I can hardly bear!
With giggles and splashes, we make quite the mess,
And the waves cheer us on—what a colorful dress!

You twirl on the sand like a kid at a fair,
But in swirls of our laughter, I think we're a pair.
With palettes of joy reflecting on skin,
It's funny how love makes the best kind of din!

As the sun waves goodbye, we can't help but grin,
In this portrait of moments, no need to begin.
For every wild color, every silly embrace,
Is a tune of our hearts, celebrating our space!

Lanterns of Love

Under the glow of the flickering light,
Two awkward dancers begin their plight.
Tripping over toes with a giggle and grin,
They share a secret, and the chaos begins.

A firefly swoops in, a reckless fly,
With a greeting so bright, they can't pass it by.
"Did you just see that?" she questions with glee,
He replies with a chuckle, "No, it saw me!"

As the sky paints a canvas of orange and pink,
They start to ponder, "What do puppies think?"
The neighbors stare puzzled, as laughter takes flight,
Creating a symphony under the beautiful night.

With lanterns in hand, they march off with flair,
Declaring their love with wild hair in the air.
Even the stars seem to join in the fun,
As they twirl and they spin till the setting is done.

Notes of Affection in Darkness

A serenade sung, off-key and loud,
To charm a partner, he's feeling so proud.
But the offbeat rhythm gives a comical show,
As she snorts into laughter, providing the glow.

With shadows dancing on the wall, quite a sight,
He trips on a rock in the dim fading light.
"Oh, darling," she giggles, "that was such grace!"
She points at his band-aid, "What happened to your face?"

Notes written on scraps, he juggles them high,
But they fly like confetti, as they both start to cry.
"Can you catch love notes like you catch my heart?"
She says while he fumbles each delicate part.

In the world's sweet dimness, laughter reigned true,
For love isn't perfect but it's funny too.
With a wink and a nudge, the night goes to bed,
They nestle their dreams, with joy in their head.

Sweet Soliloquies at Dusk

Under the shade where the shadows collide,
Whispers transform as both lovebirds abide.
"Do clouds ever get lonely?" he asks with a stare,
She laughs and replies, "Only if they care!"

As the sun dips low, casting glimmers of pink,
Their conversations grow silly, a sweet playful brink.
"What if the moon is just cheese in disguise?"
"Oh please, that's just nonsense," she laughs till she cries.

With the crickets reciting their favorite tunes,
He wonders aloud, "Do stars wear their moons?"
She nods with a grin, "It's a cosmic ballet!"
"Now watch this," he says, "as I dance the night away!"

But he trips on a twig in a graceful charade,
"Is that your best move?" she jovially invaded.
Together they chuckle, the dusk in a swirl,
Two hearts hand-in-hand in a whimsical twirl.

Light's Final Embrace

As the day waves goodbye with a flick of its hand,
They gather together, a quirky little band.
He lights up a lantern, but it flies like a kite,
Blushing, she laughs, "Did you mean to take flight?"

With a splash of orange, then deep gloomy hues,
She flips through her phone for an awkward old view.
"Check out my dance moves!" she shares with pride,
But the meme's much funnier and she bursts inside.

"Do you think the sun needs a break from the sky?"
He grins at her wisdom, "Does it ever get shy?"
Together they ponder under the evening's caress,
Their humor igniting a beautiful mess.

As the stars peek out, they share a sweet grin,
Life's many quirks are where love begins.
In the twilight's embrace, laughter's the thread,
With smiles lighting paths, as the sun goes to bed.

Nightfall's Sweet Serenade

When the sun dips low, the sky turns red,
A frog in a tuxedo hops to bed.
He croaks a tune, a silly surprise,
While fireflies dance, oh how they rise.

The moon peeks out, a smiling face,
Inviting quick antics in this cozy space.
Two cats chase tails, like a fuzzy ballet,
As night giggles softly, inviting us to play.

Stars twinkle bright, a winking affair,
An owl hoots jokes in the cool evening air.
With shadows for company, we laugh and spin,
In the twilight's embrace, where silliness begins.

So grab your friend, and take a chance,
Join the moonlit laughter, share a dance.
For in this sweet serenade of night,
Life's laughter glows under the soft light.

Chasing Dreams in Dusk's Glow

The sky is a canvas, painted in gold,
While squirrels plot mischief, both daring and bold.
Jumping from branches like they own the place,
Chasing their dreams with an acorn chase.

Fireflies flicker, like tiny taunts,
While a raccoon rummages for midnight haunts.
He trips and tumbles, then gives a shout,
"Who left these apples all about?"

In the dusky glow, we skip and we prance,
With giggles and stories, oh what a chance!
We're just two goofballs, making a scene,
In the hilarious game of the night's routine.

As dreams unfold in the night's embrace,
Laughter dances on each funny face.
So come join the fun in the twilight's flow,
As we run after dreams in dusk's warm glow.

Between Day and Night

Between the light and the dark we play,
Chasing a breeze that teases the day.
A squirrel in shades says, "You can't catch me!"
As we tumble and roll, wild and free.

With owls as judges in this silly game,
They hoot with laughter, never feeling shame.
A bat flies by in a comical swoop,
Joining our race as we form a group.

The sun winks out, it's getting late,
But who can resist this playful fate?
With chuckles and giggles, we leap and spin,
Between daylight and night, the fun begins.

So grab a friend, and take to the sky,
With silly antics, let your laughter fly.
For in this space, where shadows play,
We find our joy before it slips away.

Silhouettes of Affection

Under twilight's charm, we form a line,
Creating shadows, both silly and fine.
Giggling shapes, like a wild cartoon,
Dancing and prancing to a silly tune.

A dog wearing glasses joins in the fun,
While two ducks quack jokes, oh what a run!
With faces aglow, we strike a pose,
For silliness blooms wherever it goes.

As stars emerge, in a glittery dance,
We twirl and we hop, lost in a trance.
Each silhouette a story, funny and bright,
Crafted from laughter in the soft, warm light.

So let's embrace the laughter we find,
With pets and pals, and a pinch of wine.
For as day bows out with a wink and a cheer,
We savor these moments, hilariously dear.

Afterglow of Silent Promises

The sun dips low, a golden spat,
Two lovers lean, where did they chat?
A sly grin forms, a wink is tossed,
Their secret game? Not a thought lost.

With fingers crossed, they play the tease,
His clumsy dance made her laugh with ease.
A playful nudge, a mischievous poke,
Under the warmth of the twilight cloak.

A soft breeze carries a whispered joke,
The timing's right, or is it just smoke?
He trips on air, she rolls her eyes,
Beneath the art of silly goodbyes.

As night embraces, the stars peek out,
They ponder love, yet laugh, no doubt.
The afterglow, a sweet diversion,
In silent promises, they find their version.

Breezes of Romance

Whispers fly on a breeze so light,
Their giggles echo in fading light.
A butterfly lands on her nose,
He bursts with laughter, the fun just grows.

A breeze arrives with a playful swoosh,
Her hair's a mess, a wild whoosh!
He offers help with flailing arms,
But only adds to her clumsy charms.

With silly banter and puns galore,
She dares him to dance right on the shore.
Stumbling, twirling, they both fall down,
In playful chaos, they laugh and drown.

As sun dips low, their shadows play,
In breezes of romance, they find their way.
With joy in the air and smiles so wide,
They chase twilight with hearts open wide.

Dusky Horizons of Desire

Colors mix in a dusky swirl,
He spots her grin, gives it a twirl.
A misstep leads to an awkward stance,
But still, they share a silly romance.

Her daring hat gets swept away,
He catches it, but makes a mistake.
Diving right into the sand, not neat,
They laugh as grains pile up on their feet.

In playful whispers, they conspire,
To climb the hill, their hearts afire.
But down they roll, a tangle of limbs,
With echoes of laughter and silly whims.

As daylight fades, they sit and sigh,
In dusky horizons, they dream and fly.
With silly hearts that are light as air,
In tender moments, they make the dare.

Sunsets and Secret Glances

The sun hangs low, a slouching chair,
With secret glances, they play fair.
Her sandwich flies, a seagull's feast,
They laugh aloud, forget the least.

He bumps the cooler, drinks explode,
They dance around, lighten the load.
With chips in hair and crumbs on lips,
They steal a gaze, and their hearts flip.

Sunset hues paint their foolish game,
Each stolen look, a flickering flame.
Her wink is sly, his smile is wide,
In this strange chaos, they take the ride.

As shadows stretch, the laughter swells,
In this funny dance, their heart's bells.
Sunsets grin, with secrets in tow,
In silly moments, love starts to grow.

Heartbeats at Day's End

The sun dips low, a golden ball,
Two awkward folks begin to sprawl.
One trips and falls, a funny sight,
While shadows stretch, they laugh all night.

With ice cream cones and sprinkles caught,
They share a glance, though words are naught.
A giggle bursts, a cloud of glee,
As seagulls steal their fries with glee.

The waves applaud with foamy cheer,
As they exchange a silly sneer.
To steal a glance, to poke a cheek,
As day retreats and night grows sleek.

And while the sun fades fast away,
They scheme to spill their drinks today.
A sugary rush, a playful tease,
At day's end, it's just pure bliss.

Flickers of Emotion

The sky ignites in silly hues,
Two lovers squabble—who's to lose?
A frisbee caught, a salad toss,
With every throw, they signal loss.

The aim was off—oh what a throw!
And now it flops, oh no, oh no!
A laugh erupts, they bend and sway,
Their hearts flip-flop in grand ballet.

With popcorn fights and soda sprays,
They choreograph their quirky plays.
A dance of chuckles, fools in sync,
Their goofy smiles—what do you think?

As the sun winks with golden light,
They tumble down, what a delight!
With sandy feet and ice in hand,
They're giggling at a warm summer strand.

A Dance in the Dusk

As twilight dances, they take a chance,
With two left feet, they start to prance.
They twirl and stumble, laugh through the blur,
Each spin they make, a silly stir.

The fireflies blink like disco lights,
They break the rules of all the sights.
And just when the rhythm finds a groove,
One trips the other—but who will move?

With great aplomb, they roll on ground,
Giggles and snorts are all around.
A moonlit stage for their grand show,
With every slip, their hearts' aglow.

As stars begin to twinkle bright,
They share a snack under the night.
It's chaos truly, but oh so fun,
When dusk gives way, and the dance is done!

Echoes of Affection

In the fading light, they plot and plan,
To pull a prank, a cheeky ban.
A whoopee cushion, oh what a hit,
As laughter echoes, they can't quite quit.

The salty air tastes like delight,
With goofy grins, they take to flight.
Two clumsy hearts collide and cling,
While seashells laugh at every fling.

As he tries to impress with a cool flip,
He lands face-first, oh what a trip!
She holds her stomach, can barely breathe,
In waves of giggles, they both weave.

As the sun bows low, a sight to see,
Two hearts are wild, as wild can be.
With echoes ringing till stars emerge,
It's all in fun—a joyful surge!

Twilight Revelations

As the sun dips low, we twist and twirl,
Chasing shadows with laughter, oh what a whirl!
Your hair's a mess, but who really cares?
We stumble on secrets that dance through the air.

With giggles and grins, we take to the floor,
The moon rolls its eyes and shouts, "No more!"
Yet we spin like tops, under stars we collide,
In this wild waltz of chaos, we take all in stride.

A swoon, a spin, oh what a sight,
Our happy confusion, pure love at first bite.
The twilight's embrace makes everything right,
In a world full of chuckles, we shine ever bright.

So let's toast to the evening, with all of our might,
To the joyous blunders that sparkle the night.
With every mishap, our hearts will be light,
In the warmth of the stars, everything feels just right.

Radiance of Sweet Nothings

The day waves goodbye with a wink and a grin,
We stumble on dreams where mischief begins.
Your ideas are silly, but I play along,
As we sing out loud our nonsensical song.

Your chuckle's contagious; it spreads like a flare,
In this twilight dance, with grass in our hair.
We frolic like children, carefree and spry,
Underneath the soft canvas of twilight sky.

With bright berry stains on our cheeks, we compare,
The tastiest treats of the world we might share.
The sun's last embrace paints our faces in gold,
In this silly romance, love never gets old.

So let's hold our laughter and trouble the night,
In the glow of sweet moments, everything's right.
Shouting our secrets that bubble like wine,
As we weave through the chaos, your heart's laugh is mine.

Love Under the Waning Sky

We skip rocks on water, our giggles take flight,
As the sky starts to blush, wrapping day into night.
Your shoe's lost a lace, my hat's blown away,
As we chase all those whims that turn into play.

A wobbly boat on this river of dreams,
You push, I pull, oh, it's bursting at seams!
Each splash sends ripples of laughter so bold,
Our antics, a story, forever retold.

We race the last rays of golden delight,
With butterflies tickling our imaginations bright.
As the sky fades to purple, we're caught in a spin,
In this whimsical world, there's no need to win.

Forever we'll cherish these moments we make,
Where fun is the currency, and joy's the stake.
Our hearts wrapped in twilight, we dance as we sway,
In a love that's so wacky, come what may.

Sighs Beneath the Dimming Sun

With the sun winking low, we plot our next treat,
A silly little secret that no one can beat.
Your clownish grin has my heart in a spin,
As we stumble through moments that make our heads win.

We invent our own rules for this twilight parade,
As giggles escape while our plans slowly fade.
With each playful jab, the fun never fails,
As we flirt with the breeze that carries our tales.

The evening descends in a whirl of delight,
Where silliness reigns and it feels extra right.
With our hearts taking flight as we giggle and sway,
In this dimming wonder, we frolic and play.

So here's to the smiles as the stars peek awake,
In this twilight enchantment, make no mistake.
With laughter our language, our hearts know the way,
As we cherish these moments, come what may.

Breaths in the Twilight

The sun dips low, a golden show,
Two ducks parade, in quite a flow.
A sip of soda, a fizzy laugh,
They quack a tune, a joyful gaffe.

The breeze it giggles, the trees do sway,
A squirrel dances, hip-hop ballet.
With cheesy smiles, we wave and shout,
As clouds do form a fluffy spout.

A sprinkle of sweet, cotton candy dreams,
While fireflies light with flickering beams.
We chase our shadows, darting about,
In this twilight game, there's no room for doubt.

As stars peek shyly, we crack up in jest,
This silly moment, we feel so blessed.
With brightening hearts, as day bids adieu,
Who knew twilight could be so true?

Beyond the Orange Veil

Beneath orange skies, the world feels fun,
With hats on our heads, we're ready to run.
A pogo stick bounces, someone falls flat,
Laughter erupts; what's funny is that!

In twilight's glow, the ice cream does melt,
A sticky dilemma, oh how it's felt.
As sprinkles rain down, we're covered in glee,
We toss our woes, like leaves from a tree.

With goofy grins, we clap our hands wide,
As twilight whispers, it's time for a ride.
A bike with a horn, it toots like a bird,
We waddle and giggle, our vision blurred.

As we race the sun, on a whim we decide,
To dance with the shadows, enjoy our wild ride.
With silly small steps, we hop here and there,
Life is a sketch, we're creating with flair!

Marigold Moments

In fields of marigold, we burst out laughing,
With butterflies spinning, the day's a-glad raving.
A picnic spread wide, sandwiches tag,
A seagull swoops down, with antics to brag.

The lemonade splashes, someone steals sips,
We play silly games, with dance and flips.
The sun starts to curl, in a peachy embrace,
As ants hold a meeting, they plot our next chase.

With sunset's glow painting the skies bold,
Each moment is treasured, each joke never old.
We toss out our cares, like marigold seeds,
Laughing so hard, fulfilling our needs.

As dusk settles in, under stars so bright,
We gather 'round tales, of joy and delight.
With goofy good wishes, we bid day farewell,
For each marigold moment, we'll remember so well!

Time Stands Still

In twilight's embrace, we race against time,
With jokes that tumble, like nursery rhyme.
A cat with a hat, looks prim and so grand,
We laugh at his strut, it's something unplanned.

As shadows grow long, we play hide and seek,
The moon starts to rise, with secrets to peek.
An owl hoots softly, its deep voice a thrill,
We're stuck in this moment, and time stands still.

With friends all around, we share silly dreams,
Of candy-filled rainbows, and marshmallow beams.
As giggles explode, we dance in a line,
In this twilight magic, everything's fine.

With stars as our guides, we tell tales once more,
Of mishaps and blunders, and laughter in store.
So here in this space, we won't have to run,
For time is but laughter, and laughter is fun!

Nightfall's Sweet Surrender

As the sun dips low, we dance a jig,
With our ice cream cones, we each take a swig.
The seagull steals fries, oh what a sight,
We laugh till we cry, under fading light.

Oh, the stars come out, they wave and they twirl,
While we trip on our feet, and give a whirl.
A firefly buzzes, it wants to compete,
But our giggles are loud, it admits defeat.

The world seems to blend in shades of pink,
We stumble and fumble, what do you think?
A sunset romance with silly charades,
We'll forget the moment, but not the cascades.

So let the dusk roll in, we'll borrow the night,
With ice cream on noses, everything's right.
We'll cherish this chaos of laughter and cheer,
As the moon gives a wink, we find our way here.

Echoes of Daylight's Farewell

The sky paints a canvas, oh what a tease,
We launch paper boats, catching the breeze.
The last sunbeams wave, we play hide and seek,
While squirrels make faces, they're such a cheek!

Our sandwiches tumble, oh what a mess,
With ants joining in, who could guess?
We giggle at shadows that dance on the ground,
While the crickets chorus their nightly sound.

Butterflies flutter, they join in our fun,
We sway and we twirl as the day comes undone.
With laughter like bubbles, we float in the air,
Chasing the daylight with no single care.

And when twilight approaches, we don our best grins,
Trading small secrets and silly spin wins.
With memories made of joy, loud and clear,
We'll treasure these echoes, year after year.

Whispers of Twilight

The horizon whispers, 'Come play tag with me!'
We tumble through daisies, and giggle with glee.
A breeze tickles noses, how can we resist?
Chasing the twilight, oh, what fun we've missed!

The moon peeks out, with its shy little grin,
We dare it to dance, let the games begin!
With flips and with flops, our shadow blurs glow,
In the game of the evening, we steal the show.

The stars start to twinkle, a soft little tease,
As we spin in the grass, with the greatest of ease.
The night opens up, like a grand old book,
And we laugh at the stories, with every nook.

So here's to the twilight, that playful old friend,
When adventures abound, and laughter won't end.
With secrets we share, as bright as the sky,
We'll dance under starlight, just you and I!

Embrace of Dusk

Dusk tiptoes in with a hop and a skip,
While we launch our dreams on a wobbly ship.
The clouds do a tango, casting shadows wide,
We giggle like children, with nowhere to hide.

The sun's last hurrah, a grand swirly twirl,
Our ice cream melts down, a sugary whirl.
While the fireflies wink, we make silly poses,
Who knew the dusk brought out all these roses?

With laughter escaping like bubbles in air,
We dodge every sunset, no worry, no care.
A world full of dreams painted purple and gold,
In the embrace of twilight, warm, bright, and bold.

So dance me through dusk, with your whimsical ways,
We'll twirl with the stars, through this marshmallow haze.

With laughter our anchor, let's drift through the night,
In a silly adventure, everything feels right.